ANN MORRIS

HATS · HATS · HATS

PHOTOGRAPHS BY
KEN HEYMAN

LOTHROP, LEE & SHEPARD BOOKS
NEW YORK

Text copyright © 1989 by Ann Morris
Photographs copyright © 1989 by Ken Heyman
All rights reserved. No part of this book may be reproduced or utilized in any form or by any means, electronic
or mechanical, including photocopying, recording or by any information storage and retrieval system, with-
out permission in writing from the Publisher. Inquiries should be addressed to Lothrop, Lee & Shepard Books,
a division of William Morrow & Company, Inc., 105 Madison Avenue, New York, New York 10016.

Printed in the United States of America.
Book design by Sylvia Frezzolini
First Edition

1   2   3   4   5   6   7   8   9   10

Library of Congress Cataloging in Publication Data
Morris, Ann, Hats, hats, hats.
Summary: Introduces a variety of hats, from soft and hard hats to snuggly and hooded hats. 1. Hats—
Juvenile literature.   [1. Hats]   I. Heyman, Ken, ill.   II. Title.   TT655.M674   1989   391′.43   88-26676
ISBN 0-688-06338-1   ISBN 0-688-06339-X (lib. bdg.)

HATS · HATS · HATS

The world is
full of hats.

Soft hats

Hard hats

Sun hats

14

Fun hats

Work hats

Play hats

Ten-gallon cowboy hats

Snuggly
warm hats

23

Scarves and hoods make hats too.

Cover the head

Beautiful!

INDEX

15 UNITED STATES: An Ohio traveling circus is home for this clown who always wears a flower in his hat.

16 UNITED STATES: A New York City policewoman talking to children on her beat.

16 INDONESIA: The workers in this wheat field in Bali are carrying winnowing baskets on their heads. The baskets will be used to separate the wheat from the chaff.

17 FRANCE: These chefs' hats are similar to those worn in monasteries during the French Revolution, when chefs fled with their employers to the monasteries for safety.

18 UNITED STATES: The girl's riding hat is hard and will protect her head if she falls. She is riding English saddle. The boy wears a soft cowboy-style hat and is riding Western saddle.

19 UNITED STATES: A Fourth of July baseball game! The *B* on the hats stands for Bombers, the name of the team.

20 UNITED STATES: Ten-gallon hats are said to be big enough to hold ten gallons of water. Cowboys used their hats to water their horses when they were out on the trail.

22 EL SALVADOR: This mother shells corn while holding her warmly wrapped baby.

23 DENMARK: Danish winters are long and cold, and every Danish child must be warmly bundled up.

23 PERU: Even though this baby doesn't seem to be enjoying it, he is well protected by his handwoven blanket and cap. The shape of the mother's hat allows her to carry large objects on her head.

24 UNITED STATES: Scarves make excellent fold-up hats. Women, and sometimes men, from many countries have used scarves as head coverings for centuries.

25 UNITED STATES: These twins are cozy and warm in hoods that are attached to their snow jackets.

26 INDIA: Many kinds of head coverings can be seen at this marketplace. Colorful clothing is usually worn in the countryside. White clothing is more often worn in the city.

28 NIGERIA: These distinctive hats are made from chicken feathers and are worn by dancers who are celebrating Nigeria's independence.

29 JAPAN: This young Japanese girl wears a traditional ceremonial hat during a holiday celebration held in Kyoto.

◆◆◆◆◆◆◆◆◆◆◆◆◆◆◆◆◆◆◆ **ANN MORRIS** ◆◆◆◆◆◆◆◆◆◆◆◆◆◆◆◆◆◆◆

has taught young children in both private and public New York City schools, and has also taught at Teachers College, Columbia University; New York University; and Bank Street College of Education. She left the teaching field to become editorial director of the Early Childhood Department of Scholastic, Inc., where she produced a number of award-winning films, film-strips, and other audiovisual materials. She now devotes full time to writing and developing children's books. Among her recent titles are *Night Counting, Sleepy Sleepy,* and *Cuddle Up.*

◆◆◆◆◆◆◆◆◆◆◆◆◆◆◆◆◆◆◆ **KEN HEYMAN** ◆◆◆◆◆◆◆◆◆◆◆◆◆◆◆◆◆◆◆

is widely recognized as a foremost photojournalist. A student of Margaret Mead, he coauthored two books with her, *Family* and *World Enough.* His photographs have appeared in many other books, including *The Family of Children*, a book about childhood around the world, and *The World's Family.* His photographs in these books have earned him the reputation as one of the world's most sensitive interpreters of the human condition.